BRIGADOON CREEK

LEN HARRIS

Lovstad Publishing
Poynette, Wisconsin
www.Lovstadpublishing.com

ISBN: 0692256288
ISBN-13: 978-0692256282

Printed in the United States of America

Cover design by Lovstad Publishing
Cover photo by Mike Sepelak
Inside photos by Luke Annear and Brian Waldner

DEDICATION

All trout anglers are dreamers.
My stories are my journey through life. Some of my choices
were less than stellar and I am lucky to be alive.
My best choice of my life was marrying my beautiful wife Barb.
I dedicate this book to the love of my life Barbara Harris.
I love you honey, and the journey would have been very hollow
without you by my side to enjoy it together.

Thank you to Mike Sepelak for the beautiful cover photo.
Thank you to Luke Annear and Brian Waldner
for inside photos.
Thank you to Charlie Preusser for encouraging me
to keep writing long ago.

CONTENTS

BRIGADOON
CREEK

Brigadoon Creek

All outdoors folks have dreams of the perfect deer hunting place where the twelve point bucks are plentiful and there is a stream that runs through the center of it with many eager trout. The area must be remote and not hunted much and devoid of other anglers. Hardcore trout anglers have a lifelong quest for such a spot.

This stream may have a correct name for the dreamers but it is typically not called by name by these secretive trout nuts. It is whispered and coveted by these protectors of the trout grail. Most would give you their first born child before they divulge their "Brigadoon" creek. Every county has a Brigadoon Creek.

For those of you that are not familiar with the term "Brigadoon" creek I will elaborate. Every trout angler worth their salt is in search of the perfect stream their entire lives. If they think they have found it they replace the real name of the stream to hide its location in case prying ears ever hear them talk about it.

The origin of the "Brigadoon" handle comes from an old movie. Brigadoon was a village in the mountains that only appeared once every one hundred years. It stayed for a day and then disappeared for another hundred years. This made the Scottish town virtually impossible to visit twice in a lifetime. It was an unspoiled place. The village was from the olden days. The folks were simple folks and were satisfied with their life. The place was mythical and only dreamers dare imagined it.

Last year about this time I had brunch in New Glarus with my family. I typically go to New Glarus every weekend that there is a FREE fishing weekend. Wisconsin has this so out of state anglers can come and fish Wisconsin without having to buy a license. The streams were typically overrun with anglers on this weekend and I pass on trout fishing elbow to elbow. Everything was going like normal at the Swiss restaurant. The food was great and the ambiance was even better. My wife and I were sitting there soaking in the Swiss heritage and the excellent food when it happened.

Two white haired gentlemen sat in the booth along side of us. I guess both of them in their late 80s. These men had not seen one another for decades and were talking about everything under the sun. I listened to their conversation as I ate. The two talked about friends that had passed and their escapades as young adults. The conversation then changed to a subject dear to my heart. These two old sages were talking about trout fishing. I quietly told my family to keep their volume down because I wanted to hear what these two old trout slayers were talking about.

I felt a little bad about listening to their trout stories without them knowing but I was enthralled with what they were talking about. They were talking about their "Brigadoon Creek" that they had discovered as children. They stumbled on it by accident. There were trout everywhere. It had steep walls, almost like canyon walls that were formed over hundreds or thousands of years and it was a mini version of Rock Creek in MT.

I tried my hardest to hear where this mythical stream was. I gleaned from their conversation it was close to New Glarus. They didn't even fish the upper section where it forks to the left and goes into a secluded roadless area that is completely untouched. My curiosity got the best of me and I stood up and introduced myself to the two ancient anglers.

Brunch lasted much longer than typical that day. The two long ago gave up trout fishing and they were pleasant and they gave up the location of their "Brigadoon Creek." We shook hands and I thanked them for their valuable information. One of the old sentinels of trout told me to take a net with me because I would need it. The other told me the stream even fished better in the fall due to the big trout migrating to the stream to spawn.

3

The drive home was long. My wife and I were skeptical about the actual location of this Montana like stream in Southern Wisconsin. The next day I went on a quest to find the stream of dreams. It was quite a drive and after three hours of searching I couldn't find it. I went home defeated. I stored this information in my log book for 2012 and moved on. A couple days ago I re-read my logs for 2012 and I decided to search a little more for this trout nirvana. My wife and I went over some maps and we decided I was one valley over too far. Brigadoon Creek was there and another crusade to the stream was needed.

I hit the road at 4:30am this morning. The sun was up for about 40 minutes when I arrived. This magical stream was a tributary of a well known creek in the area. My directions from goggle maps said 500 yards upstream from the bridge it fed in to the main branch. I walked for 2,000 yards upstream and all I found was an old dry creek bed. I was a little angry at first but then I did eavesdrop on the conversation so I had no right to be mad. Maybe the dry creek bed was Brigadoon Creek and I just need to wait another 100 years before it appears again.

The fact that Brigadoon Creek only appear once every 100 years makes it impossible for any angler to visit this mythical and magical place more than one time in a lifetime.

We trout anglers are dreamers. I will find my own Brigadoon Creek someday.

RIDICULOUSNESS

Here I sit at my kitchen table. I am recuperating from back surgery. I had my L4 and L5 vertebra fused together with four titanium screws and a plate. The surgery was required due to my back wearing out. It wasn't from some childhood injury or a car accident. It easily could have been from a myriad of bad choices or simply not thinking as a kid and young adult.

This story was prompted by watching an episode of "Ridiculousness" last night with my daughter and wife. For those of you that don't know the show, it is a conglomerate of videos from YouTube of absolutely idiotic and dangerous things folks have taped and placed on the internet.

Many of the people in the show have to have been seriously injured but the show's editors chose to leave that out.

My youth was one non-stop episode from this television show. I was from a family of six kids. Being the only male my mother worried less about me. My father died when I was ten years old and I was basically without adult supervision from age ten until I was twenty years old and went into the Army.

Some of my less than stellar decisions as a kid, I blame on stupidity and others I rack up to "What doesn't kill you makes you stronger." If there are any kids reading this story please heed my tales of misfortune and don't try to repeat them.

I am going to begin my wayward trek with just a plain and simple accident. It was the first day the swimming pool was open in Gays Mills. I guess June 14th, 1968 as the day. It was a day after my birthday and I was on my way to the pool sporting a new huge bath towel and my blinged out new Green Bay Packers flip flops.

The spring floods had shifted the small bridge at the base of the hill just before the pool and there was not a route up the hill without wading across the small creek. I didn't want to dirty my new Packer flip flops before I could show them off at the pool. I decided I would crawl up on the rail and balance on it and walk across and jump off the rail at the end to avoid the water. It all worked out as planned. I made one mighty jump at the end to clear the water. I struck the landing. I was a little proud of myself for the feat.

Off I went to the pool. I took one step forward with my left foot and tried an accompanying right step but my right foot wouldn't move. It was like it was cemented to the ground. I knelt down to examine what was going on.

I saw a sharp thing protruding from the center of the top of my right foot. I tipped my foot to the side and then the pain hit me. I had jumped off that rail on top of another piece of two-by-four that was about four feet long. The board had a giant nail in it and it was now completely through my entire foot. My first impulse was to try to pull it off but that wasn't happening. No one was at the pool. I wanted to be there first and I was. I was all alone.

I limped home twelve blocks with that board welded to my foot. A fast trip to the ER and a tetanus shot and I was good to go. My new flip flops had to be cut off to extract the nail and my new beach towel was a mess due to bleeding all twelve blocks home. The horror stories keep on rolling throughout my youth.

Fall came quickly and that meant going to the dump to search for treasure with my good friend John. The treasure hunt was less than stellar that day and we decided to get a 55 gallon drum and fill it with magazines and see what we could melt in there with our raging inferno. It was amazing at what would melt if we got the fire burning hot enough. That grew boring quite quickly so we decided to throw in aerosol cans. We took turns throwing them in and running like crazy to get away from the potential missile or grenade effect. Some of those spray paint cans really rocked the surroundings dump and woods when they exploded; it was like World War Two.

Our eleven year old brains obviously didn't register the real danger we were putting ourselves into. Some of the hair spray cans that were full really shot up high in the air before exploding. It was my turn and I had found an almost full Aquanet can and I bragged to John that I bet this would be the best yet.

John got extra far away from the burning barrel and hid behind an old junk car. I tossed the can in and hauled butt to my area of cover. I did not make it there. I saw a fireball go directly in front of my eyes and a giant explosion just 20 feet from me. John ran to me and was frantic and asked me if I was okay. I didn't know what all the fuss was about until John told me what he saw.

He told me that the Aquanet can came out of the fire almost as fast as I threw it in and came screaming out of the inferno right at my head like a guided missile. He was certain it had hit me in the head. We did a check of my head for injuries. Both of my eyebrows and eye lashes were burnt off. That missile had missed my head by literally an eye lash. John and I swore each other to secrecy and moved on with our less than brilliant childhoods.

Spring came quickly and so did my stupidity. Another friend of mine and I hung out a lot when we were young. I am going to leave his name out of the story because it might embarrass him. We were at the playground in Gays Mills. The regular playground equipment grew boring really quickly so we moved back towards the river and swamp behind the playground. All of you know what a telephone pole looks like. Some of them have a metal cable that anchors them in place. It runs from the ground to the top of the pole at an angle and is secured to the ground with a metal spike and to the top of the pole with a loop. This cable was not tight like typical cables are. It had some slack in it. I was the first to swing around on it like

"George of the Jungle."

That was a popular cartoon during those times. My friend and I always had a friendly competition going on about almost everything and this was no different so we tried to see who could swing more times around the cable. I was a really scrawny kid. My buddy was a little heavier and a little stronger than me and typically won most of our competitions.   I was watching him spin around the cable and he was claiming his championship of the "George of the Jungle" when it happened.

Because he was just a little heavier than I was, he caused the cable to swing wider and the cable touched the two leads of the transformer on the top of the pole. What happened next was surreal. The cable touching the transformer caused what looked like a lightning bolt of blue and yellow fire to travel down the cable. It happened so quickly my friend was unable to let go. His body straightened out like a board and he was thrown twenty feet.

The sparks were flying at the top of the pole and the transformer exploded. Sparks were raining down on both of us and I was scared for my friend. I went to see if I could help him. Before I could get to him he popped up off the ground and ran home at Mach 12.

I later learned that he was not killed because of the giant amount of power that came down that wire caused him to be thrown free instead of locking him in place and him becoming another statistic. I am very glad that I did not win that George of the Jungle competition that day.

Then there was the "Mad Bomber" hat. I saw some older kid with one and I had to have one and begged almost a year for it. My mom finally gave in and bought one for me for Christmas. It was rabbit fur lined. It looked kind of like a Russian military hat. You could fold the ear flaps up. It depended on how warm of a day it was. It was a warm December day so I folded up the ear flaps and clipped them above my head. Off I went to my favorite fishing place and was casting away. This is where the story gets a little dicey. I don't remember any of it. From what the doctor told me I was a very lucky young man.

A semi-truck had driven by where I was fishing and a rock had squirted out the side of the tire as it ran over it. The rock catapulted at me. My back was turned facing the water. The small rock hit me on the back of the head and knocked me out. The next driver going by saw me in a heap and called for help. If I had not folded up that cap and gave myself a double layer of protection that day, I would have died from the blow to the head. I got knocked out cold. If I would have fallen into the Kickapoo River I would have drowned that day.

There have been lots of close calls for me throughout my life. Some involved bees. Other involved being submerged in a full septic tank. There was a couple throwing bottles at signs incidents that required sutures. I will leave you with the last less than intelligent choice I can remember.

I was home on leave from the Army. It was my first leave after basic training. I was lean and mean and full of myself. My brother in law Dennis and I went out celebrating. It was three o'clock in the morning and I decided I wanted to take a swim at the local dam. I took off my glasses and new Mickey Mouse watch and took my wallet out of my pocket and placed them on the flood gate.

Dennis didn't swim so he watched from above the dam. Dennis was actually terrified of water so I was messing with him. The dam in Gays Mills has taken a few lives in its day when the water was high. This time it was as low as I had ever seen it. As a young whipper snapper I had slid off the dam many times. There is a proper way to slide off and then there is the head first way. Head first usually meant you were knocked out and a dirt nap followed very shortly.

I decided to tease Dennis and hid in an area he couldn't see me just to mess with him. He yelled for me a couple times and I did not respond. The neighbors must have been woken up by my yelling and Dennis yelling and me not responding. The next thing I knew the Sheriff's Department and Rescue Squad arrived. I scurried up the flood gate to put my glasses on and retrieve my watch and wallet. All were gone. In Dennis' frantic search for me he had kicked them in the water and they were long gone. We explained to the police what was going on. Later that week I received a huge bill for the police and rescue being called out at three a.m. Before I left to Germany on my first assignment, I stopped at the store and bought another Mick Mouse watch. I got my new glasses the day before I shipped out.

An Ugly Place

My memory works too well some of the time. I am the person in the photo. I believe it was my wife taking the photo. The photographer is the only thing I don't remember. My old catch phrase was not working this day. Back when I did presentations at schools, I use to call the power point: *"Trout Don't Live In Ugly Places."* This day the opposite was the norm. The banks were terribly eroded and cows had pulverized the banks. My expectations were low this day.

It was early season in Crawford County. I was crossing the stream because the hole in the distance was a ninety degree bend and I had caught a couple decent browns and brooks in the bend about fifty yards upstream. When I got in the water, the loose sediment on the bottom made a huge cloud downstream and I frowned. Typically when there is lots of loose sediment on the bottom there are not many invertebrates in the waterway. For you non-trout savvy folk, the invertebrates' word in layman's terms is food or little bugs and water creatures for the trout to eat.

There were cows all over the place and I am allergic to bulls so I was looking to see if any of these bigger cows were sporting any hardware. All of them looked like udders so I was about to cross the electric fence when the weirdest feeling come over me. It was like a subliminal message. I heard: "Look to your left dummy."

The water I was standing in was maybe two inches deep but there was a downed tree laying on the electric fence on the left. That tree had roots that stuck up in the air a ways so I thought the roots under the water must at least be that long creating an 18 to 24 inch cut out underneath. I thought about the sediment flying up when I crossed and all that I have read in books by the masters of trout fishing and decided I was going to cast above the roots anyway.

My first cast was an epic fail on a side arm cast under the electric fence. It landed about two feet from the root wad. Instead of reeling it in I just gave the rod a tug and reeled in my short, not on target cast. My tug caused quite a commotion near that root wad. There was a huge swirl there and I smiled and thought about all *the know it alls* in those fly fishing magazines and on the internet. Something was there and it wanted my Panther Martin.

I crouched down and did a better sidearm cast upstream of the roots. I didn't want my cast to scare my prey and I wanted the spinner to come down naturally like food. I brought the size nine Panther Martin brown trout pattern right next to the root wad. There were no takers. I continued to reel and then I saw its back come up out of the water and it followed my lure nearly to my feet and it slammed the lure in two inches of water. Three quarters of its body was out of the water when it hit. The trout thrashing was quite a sight to the photographer. He came screaming down the bank and netted the nice male brown for me.

Now that I think about it. It was not my wife that took this photo; it was Aaron Wachtendonk. I snapped a couple of photos of the trout and let it go due to it being mandatory catch and release in early season in Wisconsin. The big male brown had inhaled my barbless spinner and he was bleeding badly when I let him go. He swam off really quickly but I am certain he died at a later time due to blood loss. I truly hate mandatory catch and release season because of exactly what happened to me. If trout are going to die they should not be released. It is wanton waste of our resources. My wife Barb calls early season "Torture and Release" season, and equates it to golfing using a chipmunk for the ball.

Because I caught a trout, Aaron was up to bat. He couldn't get another one out of the electric fence hole so we moved upstream. When I fish with someone there is an unwritten rule that says fish until you catch or lose one and then it is the next person's turn to fish again.

The spring floods had carved quite a funnel on the left bank that wasn't there the year before. Deep funnels are typically fast water and on the downhill grade we were fishing, the probability of catching a nice fish was really low. Aaron struck out his first couple casts. Fast water in early season typically doesn't work well. The water is too cold and the trout need to expend lots of energy to hold in place in frigid water and the reward versus effort wasn't in the trout's favor.

We only walked ten yards upstream and there it was in the fast moving trench-like area the spring floods had created! There was a really nice boulder in the water. This would be the perfect place for a trout to hide behind and be out of the fast cold water and still have a bird's eye view of food going past. Aaron cast upstream about five yards above the boulder with his Panther Martin and ran the barbless spinner right by the slow side of the boulder. His effort was rewarded with the biggest brook trout he has ever caught in his lifetime.

The moral of the story is that trout do live in ugly places some of the time. Also don't let the folks that write all the trout fishing books use their expertise to dissuade you from catching the biggest brook trout of your lifetime.

A WARM AND WINDY DAY IN MAY

I t was a late May 2012 in southwestern Wisconsin. It was unusually warm for May. There was an odd wind coming out of the northwest. Typically winds from the northwest this time of the year were cold. The temperature rose about ten degrees warmer than the day before. The warm up intrigued me. I thought the trout may turn on because of it. I hurried home to get my gear and get out fishing.

It was mid afternoon by the time I hit the stream. The wind was warm but a little too gusty at times. My casts were not the best at the beginning of the outing and I ended up in the trees a couple times. But I didn't feel frustrated on this warm day in May with the wind in my face and a rod in my hand. The ground was still quite soft from the winter melt off. I decided to take the good with the bad and continue on. The trout were eager when I did get a good cast in.

The stretch I picked was a long one. It was owned by three different landowners. I had permission on the beginning and ending stretch. The middle section was a wade-only stretch. I finished the middle stretch and the last stretch opened before me. It was wide open with a fallow pasture. The cows had not manicured the grass yet. The grass was about mid-thigh high. I was happy to get out of the water and walk stream side.

There was a cow path on the edge of the stream that I used because I was a little tired from the long walk. The path had some wear but it was not beaten down like years past. I was up higher out of the stream and could see much better ahead of me. The wind became a factor again and the chop on the water was bad. I actually was enjoying the odd wind in my face and the smells of the stream. It was refreshing because of the long winter. I had to time my casts between gusts. It seemed to work well. It was getting late in the afternoon and it was overcast. I kept telling myself: "This is my last cast. If I get a decent trout I will quit for the day." I trudged on for that one last decent trout.

I saw movement in the grass about twenty feet ahead of me. Fishing abruptly became secondary and my gaze focused on the movement in the tall grass. I was not sure what I was looking at to begin with. I thought I had walked up on a possum or a raccoon because I could only see a little fur through the tall grass. Things changed very quickly.

I then saw a furry ear rise up out of the grass. My first thought was I had found a dog in the grass taking a nap. My past encounters with dogs on streams were varied. I reached down to my left side for my bear pepper spray. Before I could pull the spray out of the carrier it appeared in its entirety in front of me. I froze in my tracks and didn't move a muscle.

The front end of the creature lifted up and then I saw its rear end and tail. It stretched like I had seen many dogs do when awoken from a nap. It was facing away from me and it was not a dog. I attempted to secure my pepper spray again. My hands were shaking very badly now. There was an adult wolf standing twenty feet from me and it had not seen me yet.

The wolf looked darker than I had seen photos of and much larger. I had watched "The Gray" movie that spring and all the bad scenes of the movie flashed before me. I was petrified with fear. My strong hand had a hold of my fishing rod. For some crazy reason I had not dropped it while trying to get the pepper spray. I was flailing with my left hand in an attempt to get the spray. I questioned my-self for the placement of the pepper spray on my left hip. I had it there because it interfered with my casting on my right hip. I did not want to take my eyes off the wolf. Then it happened.

The wolf took one step forward and turned and looked right at me. I was not sure why it turned and looked at me but I was certain later that it could hear my heart beating a hundred miles an hour and almost bursting out of my chest. It squared itself and looked directly at me. I was in a trance. I could not move.

I saw its ears go back and the hair on its back stood up. It slightly dropped its back legs. Its stare was terrifying. It was so close I could see that it had a wet nose. I finally quit being a deer in the headlights and dropped my pole and reached with my right hand slowly to my pepper spray. The whole time I was keeping a close eye on the wolf. I could not secure the pepper spray without looking at it. The description of the events makes it sound like I was staring at this wolf for ten or fifteen minutes when it was only ten or fifteen seconds. Ten seconds is much too long in my opinion.

Pepper spray was my only defense and I needed it now! I dropped my eyes to my hip to secure the spray and got it quickly. Next I had to get the safety button off. This went by in an instant because I had practiced this. I had it up and armed and was pointing where the wolf had been. It was gone. When I broke eye contact with it, the wolf must have seen that as its opportunity to run. I did a 360 quickly to make sure it wasn't flanking me. It was nowhere to be seen. I picked up my rod quickly and side-stepped left traveling out of the field.

Each time the wind blew it made me think something was coming for me when the grass moved. The stories of my youth that involved the big bad wolf were flashing through my mind. I thought that where there was one wolf, there might be more. The sideways walking to the road seemed to take forever. I did not want to turn my back to where I had last seen the wolf.

My thoughts were rambling. It came to me that the wolf was sleeping with its face to the wind to be alerted to danger. The wind and the soft earth made my approach silent and without a scent to alert. I evaluated my reactions to the wolf. I was not pleased with my locking up under stress. If I had sprayed the pepper spray at the wolf I would have indirectly sprayed myself in the face due to the wind. I decided that a pepper flavored human may not taste well to wolves so if one attacked I was going to empty the canister.

I was finally on the road walking back to my truck. I checked behind myself quite often and my pace was almost a jog. It seemed like it took forever to get to the vehicle and get the door closed. I sat there for a short time getting my shit together. My heart was still racing and trying to erupt from my chest. I decided on the way home I was not going to tell my daughter and wife about my close encounter.

I did not return to that stretch that year. I started to pester my wife about buying a pistol for self defense and for carrying on stream for my safety. She vetoed the purchase of a pistol for three months until I told her a short version of this story. I purchased a pistol online the same day and had my concealed carry permit three weeks later. This was early November. Trout season was closed.

During the closed season I practiced with my pistol. I had purchased a shoulder holster for my 357 magnum. I picked a revolver because of my law enforcement background. A pistol that may become wet while wading during fishing needs to be dependable. Revolvers are much less apt to jam than an automatic. My pistol is a short barreled version so as not to hinder drawing it quickly in a stressful situation. The shorter barrel also makes the pistol much louder than typical so the sound of the pistol would also be a deterrent.

I later sold the 357 due to it having too small of a handle. In a stressful situation you want control of your pistol. I purchased another Ruger pistol. This one is a 44 magnum. What sold me on this model was the pistol is used by guides in Alaska for self defense against grizzlies. The pistol is called an Alaskan and has the same short barrel. I am much more accurate with this pistol. I also wore my bear pepper spray on my right hip after the close encounter with the wolf instead of the left.

I know there are some folks cringing when they read this story. Some are scared like I was and others think my fear is unsubstantiated and are critical. I don't kill animals for sport. My gun is for personal defense and you weren't in my shoes on a warm windy day in May with a wolf literally feet away!

AN OPENER TO REMEMBER

Years fly by these days but I knew this was an opener the spring after I discovered this hole. I arrived a little too early this day and had to wait two hours to fish it before the shell ice came off of it.

There was fresh snow and the waiting for the shell ice to go off almost drove me crazy. I was not comfortable casting into the hole until almost 11 a.m. because of that ice. This spot had all the markings of a perfect wintering hole. There was a fast feed lane at the top and a serious step drop for the trout to hide under to ambush their prey.

I needed to wade out in to the still water at the back of the pool to get up far enough in the pool to cast above the fast water so my spinner splash didn't scare the residents of this hole. I had fished the hole the year before and had excellent luck. The hole produced a twenty seven and three quarters inch female brown that year.

I needed to go down side arm to get under the low hanging limbs at the top of the hole. I had thought about these limbs the night before opener. I had already practiced my side arm casts on the way to the hole.

My side arm cast practice had produced a hook jawed brown on a hole below the bridge ruins. This was an opener and I usually have a superstition about stopping when I catch a trout over twenty inches but today felt special. A quick measure and photo of a twenty three inch brown was completed and back he went in to his cut corner under the low hanging limbs.

The water was still so I needed to wade up without throwing a wake at the fish and scare them. A wake in a calm hole is like yelling at the trout and alerting them. I slow waded about fifteen minutes to cover twenty feet. The water was maybe just below my knees after the wade. The bottom was made of small rock. This was a perfect bottom for invertebrates and minnows to thrive in. The slow wade up was endless but I finally made it there.

My first cast was true and a hook up was immediate. A seventeen incher put up quite a battle. I immediately fought her downstream away from the meat of the hole so I could catch another fish on other casts. I didn't want her to spook the hole. One photo and a measure and she was let go downstream of the hole. I was a little disappointed my cast didn't bring a bigger fish.

I repositioned myself with that slow wade not to spook the fish and then I stood there a little to let the area calm down. I cast in there again and bang there was another. The nineteen inch female fought like a bigger fish but she made it to the net and for a photo and was let go down stream. I think she fought bigger because of her huge tail. It gave her more leverage.

I typically let trout go 10-15 yards downstream of a big hole. I don't want them to scurry back in there and tell the others with their body language that they are upset. I made the slow walk up again in to the hole. I waited again and cast in the hole for third time. The third cast was true but nobody was home.

I adjusted my sight picture and decided the right side had a dead spot in the current that might hold a nice fish. There were overhanging limbs again so my side arm cast was needed. The fourth cast was golden. This fish had some shoulders and took me deep and refused to surface. It ran around the hole for quite some time before it came to net.

He measured twenty one inches and was let go back in the main hole. I quit opening day that year and went home. Not a bad opener.....about 30 casts and four big trout measuring seventeen, nineteen, twenty one and twenty three inches. My net opening is exactly twenty inches and this is how I made my quick measurements.

I have kept log books now for about 25 years and I had my best numbers ever last year but by far my worst big fish year ever. I am sorry to say the years of big trout have ended and the numbers years are upon us. Trout are being managed differently by the WDNR and has made our streams overrun with many stunted little fish. There is only so much food available for trout to eat. If you put more in the same space you have a slower growth rate due to lack of food. Do old trout anglers a favor please? Keep a few more trout in future so the herd can be thinned and the big trout can return.

CHESS MATCH WITH HUGE PIKE

Last January I was at the dam in Gays Mills throwing around some spoons trying to get a pike to come and play and I saw the most awe inspiring thing I have ever seen while pike fishing.

The carp typically school up below the first dam on the Kickapoo River every winter. This is right in my hometown of Gays Mills. These schooling carp have an interesting secondary effect. The smaller carp attract the big predators like pike.

Getting back to casting my little cleo for a wayward pike. I was there about ten minutes. The carp were schooled up in the open water just below the dam like usual. There had to be 300-400 carp schooled there. There was every size imaginable carp there. I typically work the edges of the carp to get a pike to play.

Then it happened. The water is typically really clear there and I can see down a good eight feet. The carp all parted quickly. It was like the Red Seas being parted in the bible. The only difference was there was no bearded guy with a long staff parting the carp. There was an enormous pike parting the school of carp with a smallish carp sideways in its mouth. I swear I could hear the jaws tune playing. My biggest pike to date is 41 inches. This pike had that one by about 6 inches or so. It was so wide across the head I was left with my knees shaking. I guess the monster at 48 inches and 30 pounds. She did not come back that day. May season opened on the 4th and the water was high and dirty. Not many people went to the dam to fish because of it.

The Wednesday after the opener the water was down and a little cleaner. So I decided it was time to try the HUGE pike. I had gone to Cabela's during the closed season and stocked up on lures I thought the monster would like. I had new 30 pound power pro on my Shimano 4000 reel and inspected my Falcon medium heavy spinning rod and was ready to dance with the big girl.

My second cast in to the dam area was rewarded with a follow by the resident monster. She looked like a mini submarine turning at shore. I threw right back in there and my lure was freight trained. It was a relativity short battle. I landed a nice 38 incher. It still boggles my mind that I was actually disappointed in a 38 inch pike. No more takers that day. How is it possible that I was disappointed in a pike of this size?

Mother's Day was last Sunday and I was in my hometown so I broke away from the family and went to the Kickapoo to try again. I cast and cast for almost 2 hours. I changed lures at least 20 times during those two hours. I told myself it was my last cast and I looked in my box and put on a bass lure with a white and chartreuse skirt. I was just to lift it out of the water and there she came. She hammered the lure and the one hooked lure just bounced off her armor plated mouth and swam away. No more hits after another hour of casting.

I took my daughter to school Monday morning and then drove the 32 miles to Gays Mills to try to catch the monster of the Gays Mills dam. Ten casts in my lure was slammed by a fish. This fish ran off lots of drag and it had me excited for a while. Five minutes later I landed her. It was not her. It was another nice pike but only a lowly 34 incher. No more hits after two more hours of casting.

I just got back from the dam. I cast from first light to about 8:45am. There were no hits. The weather is supposed to get really warm the next few days and cool down a little on Thursday. I plan a return trip on Thursday.

My first love will always be trout fishing. Through the years I have noticed a significant increase in the trout population. With the population increasing it has a secondary effect to the size of the trout. The days of monster trout have become quite scares these days. I am an adrenalin junky and my second love with the toothy mouths and ferocious hits are becoming more numerous. I believe the trout need to be put on the back burner for a while. I am pretty confident that my monster pike will still be around for a couple years. Pike can live to be over 20 years old. This monster I found has to be pushing 20 years old. Most people at the dam in Gays Mills throw the same exact things year after year. They typically don't have the sufficient test line to handle a 25 plus pound pike on and if they have hook ups they are left a sniffling mess after the fast snap of their line. My pike tackle box is loaded and I am ready to dance.

FIVE NEW TROUT ANGLERS
WERE BORN TODAY

I typically fish upstream. I often park my SUV at the bottom of my trout fishing water and walk back to it after fishing. I have met many a country folk on the way back to the vehicle. I usually chit chat a little with the friendly folks along the way on my sometimes long walk back.

Today was a long fishing day for me. I was in a good mood because of all of my luck and success on stream. I was slowly working my way back to my starting spot when I came upon a house whose owners I had spoken to in the past. I remember the folks as a large Mennonite family.

Dad was raking the driveway and there were four barefoot little ones running around the yard. All were fair-haired. Three little girls were in pastel colored long dresses. Their ages I guess ranged from three to six years old. There was one little boy about seven years old. The minute I started talking to their dad they all came to see what we were talking about.

They were all very quiet and respectful as we adults talked. Dad asked me if I caught any fish and I told him about my luck. All of the children looked at each other simultaneously and their eyes were as big as saucers and they had huge smiles. Dad saw their reactions and said, "I have been promising them that I would take them fishing. I even bought a rod and reel but we haven't found the time."

The father asked me the laws on him tying on lures and hooks for his kids. I gave him the rundown on the trout regulations. The father had never been fishing before and didn't know how to clean trout. That was my cue to speak up. I had two nice browns in my creel. I asked the crew if they wanted to learn how to clean trout.

We went into the yard and opened my creel by the outdoor spigot. The kids were excited but quiet when they saw the two eighteen inch trout I had in there. Dad was amazed that the stream right out his front door held such big trout. I got out my scissors from my vest. I was going to show Dad how to clean a trout. I went step by step slowly. The dad told his kids to get close and watch how to clean trout because if he was taking them fishing they needed to know how to clean fish.

It was like déjà vu for me. I flashed back to when I was five years old and cleaned my first trout. I was surrounded by my five sisters as I completed the task. These young ones were so quiet and respectful it was like going back in time. There was no screaming or pushing and I was certain they had no hand-held computer nonsense. The outdoors entertained them just like it did me and my sisters many years ago.

I took out the other trout and looked at the kids and asked, "Which of you wants to clean this trout?" There was no fighting about who was going to do it. The eldest of the four stepped up and cleaned that trout just as well as I did.

I looked at Dad and asked if they would like a couple of freshly cleaned trout. He responded right away with a yes. I told him how to prepare them. All three of the little fair-haired girls were captivated with my instructions. The father told me the girls had already had cooking lessons from their mother.

The Dad thanked me and off I walked. Two minutes later I saw him pull up with his vehicle and he offered me a ride to mine. We talked on the way and I told him a couple places in the area that his kids could catch some trout easily. Before Dad could leave I gave him four panther martins for each of his kids and some size eight eagle claws and some split shots. Five new anglers were born today. Four young ones and one Dad were turned on to the magic that is trout fishing.

KING CUTHBERT

At first glance you suspect this waterway could hold big browns and you get chills thinking about them, and you are dreaming of your drag screaming and line snapping. The only real problem with this dream is that it is reality. This short stretch of water has reduced many a sage angler into shaken blathers of witnessing unbelievable trout of sea monster proportions. I can still remember Stewart Riley telling me about his less than stellar encounter with a monster trout that he described as bigger than most steelhead he has caught.

We got out of the vehicle downstream a ways. Stew is from England and has fished the chalk streams over there and he was less than complimentary about this stretch. He called it frog water. I enlightened him that this was quality water and not quantity water. He was dying to break in his new Schroeder three weight bamboo rod his wife had given him for his birthday. I told him to leave it in the truck and a 5/6 weight rod was more appropriate for the monsters we could encounter. He did not heed my warning.

It was early season on this non-typical trout water. The banks were quite steep and this made for poor casting from them. A long handled net was required or some up close and personal wading through the mess. Stew opted for the up close and personal route.

We both had landed a couple decent browns on the stretch. I watched Stew battle a medium sized brown on his soft bamboo rod. The rod was almost bent in half and I was still of the opinion he was under gunned for the potential trout on this water. I suggested he go back and get his 5/6 weight. He declined my suggestion.

When I fish with people, I typically like showing them a good time so I decided to let Stew fish a hole that I knew a big fish lived in. Stew was trying out the hole from the east bank and wasn't really working it right. He went downstream a ways and crossed in shallow water and got down on the 90 degree bend from the other side. Stew was one of these guys that was tenacious, and a good looking hole required anywhere from 45 minutes to an hour and a half to properly cut apart. I left Stew at this hole because I was not up for waiting that long to see him fish it properly.

I looped around the hole Stew was fishing so I

wouldn't spook his potential prey. I made it back to the water about 30 yards upstream. I started casting into the log jams and snarls I was used to fishing on this stretch and heard a thunderous "LEN!!!" being shouted by Stew. This only meant one thing in my book. He had hooked a monster and needed my help landing it. I ran as fast as a big fat white man can to where I had left him.

It took a little while to get through the fallen weeds and underbrush to get to Stew. He was seated on the 90 degree bend on the other side on a soft mud delta that the spring floods had made. There was no bend in his rod or drags screaming. There he sat with his head in his hands and mumbling. The only thing that I understood from his whimpering was: "I should have listened to Len." It was obvious he had broken off on a large fish. I sat down in the tall weeds and watched him fish that hole for another 45 minutes with no takers. He finally gave up and went back downstream and crossed. I met him where he crossed. He was mumbling and he wanted to take me back to the 90 degree corner and talk. He was still visibly shaken 45 minutes after his encounter.

First thing he blurted out was: "You were right about me choosing the wrong rod." He gave me the complete skinny from how he began to how he ended. Stew typically fishes holes the same every time he fishes them. He goes bottom right and bottom middle and bottom left. He repeats the same fishing action again but with longer casts and covers more water. He had on a size eight wooly bugger with weight in the body and he was fishing without an indicator. He was dredging the bottom like I suggested when he first saw it. The first flash of the fish was "unbelievable," he muttered. He didn't get a good look at it but he was in disbelief at the size. He thought it was magnified when the fish turned up on its side in the water.

Stew has a standing operating procedure. Whenever he sees a large fish, he checks his line for wind knots and checks to see if the knot looks good. He fired right back in there after his knot check. He was a little left and off target of his prior cast so he stripped in his bugger quite quickly this time. He was cursing his poor casting as he lifted the fly out of the water when he saw it. It was two inches from his fly when Stew took it out of the water. It sat there for a micro-second and slowly swam back out into the hole. He got a really good look at it this time. Stew told me he was shaking like a school girl. He wasn't sure what to do. This trout was bigger than most steelhead he had encountered in the Great Lakes and he felt incredibly under gunned with his tiny three weight.

The car was way too far to go back to now so he adjusted his leader. He took off his 4X leader and put on a new 2X leader. He tied the same bugger on and attacked the hole again. There it was again following his bugger not ten feet in front of him. He slowed his retrieve on the next cast and it followed again. This was three times he saw this monstrous male brown. It turned off at the last minute and didn't hit. Stew fired right back in there and slowly retrieved the bi-colored bugger and the trout hit right near shore. This is when he shouted out "LEN!!" to call for me to assist.

He told me that before the shout was finished his line came back limp. He inspected the line and it was a clear cut. The steelhead sized male brown trout must have had teeth like an alligator because he barely felt any bend on his rod before the line went limp. On the way back to the vehicle I told him that such a monstrous fish should have a name. The angler that lost the fish must give it a name. Stew told me about some King from England that was a crazy trout angler. The king's name was Cuthbert and that was what he was naming his lost giant.

Stew was truly concerned about depositing the size eight bugger in Cuthbert's jaw. He worried that it might die because of the bugger in its jaw. My next comment probably soothed him and also made him weak in the knees. I said: "I didn't see that fish but the way you described the large headed monstrous male and how the line came back so fast, I seriously doubt if you got any penetration and a trout of that size has a jaw almost made of iron. I really don't think you had enough backbone in that rod to drive in the point of the hook. That trout probably spit it out as quickly as you deposited it."

We went back a couple times after Cuthbert with no takers. Cuthbert lives on in Stew's nightmares. When I asked "Stew" if I could use his name in my book, he declined. I also asked if I could use his photo and he asked me not to. Stew's name has been changed and photo modified. The loss of the biggest trout of your life must have left a scar, so I honored Stew's request to protect his identity.

LAKE LA FARGE

I n 1962, the U.S. Congress authorized construction of
a flood control dam on the Kickapoo River at La
Farge, Wisconsin. The 1,780 acre reservoir "Lake La
Farge" idea had been floating around since the 1930s.
Floating is the key word here.

Many folks saw the lake as a money making ven-
ture. Many purchased land for resorts and possible rec-
reational land on the proposed shores of the new lake.
These people were incredibly short sighted along with
Congress and the U.S. Army Corps of Engineers.

Acquisition of the property with compensation at

market value started in 1969, and ultimately 140 farms were purchased, most unwillingly from local property owners. About 9,000 acres of private property was appropriated.

In 1971, the U.S. Army Corps of Engineers broke ground on an earthen dam at La Farge. In 1975, with the dam partially in place and half of the affected highway rebuilt, a failed cost-benefit analysis led the Corps of Engineers to halt the project. Over $18 million had been spent by the time the dam project stopped.

The federal government pulled the funding because the lake they wanted to build would have had too much algae and engineers felt it wouldn't help Soldiers Grove or Gays Mills because those waters come more through Reads Creek. Viola and La Farge would have had benefit from the dam. Environmental impact statements showed many flaws in the plan. One was a potential breech and with disastrous ramifications to communities downstream.

On December 28, 2000, the deed was recorded at the Vernon County Courthouse officially transferring 7,369 acres to state ownership. The land was made into a wildlife reserve. The Kickapoo Valley Reserve is an 8,569 acre tract of land located between the villages of La Farge and Ontario in southwestern Wisconsin. A 1200-acre portion of the land has been returned to the Ho-Chunk Indian Nation, the original inhabitants of the Kickapoo Valley.

Imagine what the giant ill-conceived dam at Lake La Farge would have looked like? I grew up in Gays Mills just 33 steps from the Kickapoo River. I can remember going to sleep and water only being a little out of the banks, then waking up and getting out of bed and stepping into eight inches of water. A dam breach during the crazy floods of 2007 and the following year would have breeched the dam at Lake La Farge and washed every community in its path into the Wisconsin River.

I went into the Army in 1977 and was stationed at Yakima, Washington. The dam project was halted in 1975. I saw the flood of 1979 on the world news on television 1,400 miles away and was terrified of what happened to my mother who still lived 33 steps from the Kickapoo River. Calls home were to no avail. All phone lines were out. I eventually got a hold of the Red Cross and verified that my family was okay.

I remember shoveling 14 inches of Kickapoo River mud out of our living room once and fewer amounts on numerous other occasions. But in 1979 I was stranded in Washington State with no way to help my family this time. This was the last flood my mother would have to endure.

My mother was one of the first people to be relocated from Gays Mills by the government. The home was condemned and demolished, and my family lived in a flood relocation trailer park for a while. In 1958 my parents had purchased our home for $5,000 dollars. In 1979 my mother was given $51,000 dollars for it. My mother now has a nice home on Blue Bird Lane, far from the flood zone.

The flood of 2007 was called a 100 year flood. It was considered something that could only happen once every one hundred years. Then it happened again the following year. Can you imagine what Lake La Farge would have looked like and the communities downstream if there had been a breach to this enormous poorly contrived dam? Would you have bet your life on the control tower to keep you safe from a massive breach of that dam?

The Kickapoo River flood plain was fertile and the people that founded Gays Mills and Soldiers Grove obviously didn't think past the ends of their noses. Soldiers Grove was built for the local logging industry. The dam at Gays Mills was a mill and had zero flood control use. Soldiers Grove built a flood control dike and moved their town in 1979 before Gays Mills wised up years later.

The drought of 1988 had the water in the Kickapoo below the dam at Gays Mills the lowest I had ever seen it. I imagine Lake La Farge would not have wanted to give up any of its water because of their resorts on the shores up there and because of that, could have made the Kickapoo near Gays Mills a trickle and in turn destroying all the trout water in Crawford County.

I fish in the Kickapoo River many times a year in Gays Mills. The trout streams of the area are a large part of my life. These days a project like "Lake La Farge" would not even be considered. Can you imagine a thirty foot wall of water coming down the Kickapoo River valley, destroying everything in its path?

PARADISE CREEK

I can't remember the first time I fished Paradise Creek. It had to have been nearly fifty years ago with my father. I remember the stream well because it was where I caught my very first brook trout.

I remember my Dad saying brook trout were the most beautiful trout in the Midwest and that they were the native species. He prepared me for the outing on Paradise Creek before we went. He emphasized the beauty of the brook trout and described their neon colors to me. The look in my Dad's eyes as he talked about them showed me they had a magical quality and that he held them in high regard.

He described the brook trout as we were on the way to the stream. The first thing he painted a picture with words about was their blood red fins tipped in black and white. He said they were typically smaller trout but made up for their smaller size with ferocity. Every brookie had a unique color pattern. The worm-like swirled markings on their backs was the first thing you saw upon hook up. Then the blood red fins caught your attention as you were fighting them.

He always described wildflowers to me, and the brook trout was like a beautiful wildflower to him. The male ones had blaze orange bellies in the fall. He loved the red spots on their sides with light blue halos. His descriptions of the brook trout made them special even before I had ever fished for them.

We got out at "Paradise Creek" and I was amazed when I saw how small the stream was. I questioned my Dad and asked him if the stream got bigger. He told me "no" and this was the typical size of a brook trout stream. Brook trout needed colder water to live in and colder water meant head water and smaller streams. He then pulled two small rods from the trunk of the car. They both looked a foot shorter than what we typically fished with and the reels were smaller.

He explained that tight quarters required shorter rods and pin point casting. He explained all of this to a wide eyed seven year old and I nodded my head when he asked me if I understood, but I didn't until later in life. I do remember the tiny rod and reels and the kaleidoscope of colors I saw in my very first brook trout to hand.

One thing that stood out about that day was seeing all the beaver dams on this small stream. I could see the excitement in my Dad's eyes when we rounded a bend and saw a beaver dam. Dad always pointed out the Snake Weed or Horse Tail Rush on streams. He told me they were a good indicator of stream quality. Stream quality meant brook trout. I soon learned why as I was the first to fish that first beaver dam we encountered.

My Dad always taught me stealth was a very important thing to learn to be a good trout angler. The beaver dam hole was no different. He had me crouch down as I came up to the beaver dam a good fifteen yards before we got there. We got right down in the stream to lower our profiles. We used the beaver dam as cover. The water was gin clear and the trout had to be spooky.

My first cast over this beaver dam felt quite awkward. The spinner landed true about 25 yards up stream. I started my retrieve and the beaver dam came to life. There were at least ten wakes charging my spinner all at once. Twenty turns of the reel later I landed my first brook trout. I looked at the oddly marked fish and was in awe of its colors. My Dad's description did not do the trout justice. This trout was about eleven inches long and my Dad wowed at it as being a really big brook trout for my first ever. We put it on our stringer.

The outing screamed by and we had 20 brook trout on our stringer in no time flat. I questioned my Dad about the intelligence of this kind of trout. He held a high reverence for brook trout and I questioned it as a seven year old. Later in life I discovered why he held them in such high regard. It was that ferocity he loved and their amazing colors. He loved the tiny streams and tight quarters they lived in. They lived in the most pristine and reverent places in the outdoors. This outing later on taught me that fishing was not all about the fish. The fish were a bonus. Trout don't live in ugly places and those places needed to be enjoyed and cherished. Those places had a cleansing effect and made you appreciate the outdoors and all its wonders.

Just a few short years after this outing my Dad went to heaven to fish and I was left alone to find my own trout streams. Brook trout became scarce in the coming years. Other trout anglers blamed it on the over fishing of the species. I was still young and really didn't know the reasoning. I was certain my Dad was catching brook trout in heaven.

About twenty years ago there was a rebirth, a sort of renaissance of the brook trout population in my home waters. They were as plentiful as they once were when my Dad and I fished. It was nothing to have a hundred brook trout day a dozen years ago.

About a dozen years ago it started to happen again. My brook trout were on the decline. Then some of my streams had none at all. I stopped harvesting brook trout because of it. I examined many of the brook trout I did still catch and their gills looked different. They had some type of parasite attached to them. I contacted the

WDNR right away about eleven years ago. They dismissed my worries.

Today it is 2014 and my brook trout have all but disappeared from "Paradise Creek." The culprit has a name now and it is gill lice. The decline of the brook trout 50 years ago was not fishing pressure and over harvest. It was gill lice back then and it is gill lice now. The WDNR has no solution or magic pill to treat my brook trout.

The WDNR is recommending reporting beaver dams on trout streams. These are the breeding grounds of gill lice. The trout school up there and infect one another. The WDNR wants those locations so they can tear down those dams. They are also encouraging harvest of brook trout to cut down on their numbers. This parasite does not hurt humans and only attaches to brook trout.

The old adage of 'you don't appreciate something until it is gone' is once again true in Crawford County. Paradise Creek today is devoid of brook trout. It has a thriving population of brown trout. Gill lice are spreading all over the state.

All of you anglers that chase the elusive brook trout know of what I speak. Appreciate the streams and their residents. Enjoy yourself when on stream and drink in what nature has to offer because it could disappear twice in your lifetime.

THE CAPTAIN

M y Dad was originally from Oconto Falls. The big lakes were introduced to him at a young age. He was often either on shore fishing for salmon or lake run browns or out on a boat after them as a kid. He was devastated when he learned his family was moving off the big lake and moving to Trego, Wisconsin. His mom reassured him that they were moving to a good fishing area and there would be lots of lakes nearby to fish.

Dad quickly adjusted to the area. It helped that his mother was a Northern Pike and walleye nut and she spent many a day on Rice Lake chasing them. Dad was introduced to boats at a very young age. He motored on the lakes of northern Wisconsin by himself by age twelve.

Childhood quickly moved on to adulthood. The carefree days of his youth were replaced with learning a trade. His trade of welding and steam fitting sent him to Milwaukee to work. He needed the water close to him so he chose where jobs were aplenty and fishing was not far away. There was one constant and it was fishing somewhere or planning to go fishing somewhere.

His plans of working and fishing ran into a detour in 1949. He met my mother at a diner in Milwaukee. She was waiting tables there and caught my Dad's eye.

I will fast forward to 1958. The Harris Family was now at three daughters and me. My mother pestered my Dad about moving to a better place to raise kids. Milwaukee was just starting to be a large city and crime was beginning to get too close to their home.

Mom and Dad discussed and argued about where they were going to live. They decided to visit both the places that they had lived as kids and assess jobs and the close proximity to fishing and dad's new passion of hunting.

Dad was invited to go pheasant hunting in Gays Mills by Mom's brother. This was the first place Dad did "recon" on jobs. It happened really by total luck. Dad and my Uncle Sig were pheasant hunting near Gays Mills and Dad chatted with a guy in the parking lot. Dad was admiring the guy's lab, and ways lead on to ways and lo and behold the guy with the lab was the crew leader at Genoa Power Plant. He offered Dad a job as a welder there, about thirty miles from Gays Mills. We moved ten days later to Gays Mills.

Our new home was 33 steps from the Kickapoo River and 17 minutes by car to the Mississippi River. It took Dad two days before he had a boat and was motoring up and down the Kickapoo River and exploring the backwaters of the Mississippi. I was still too small to go with him but I watched many days as he hooked up the boat at first light and came back after dark.

Then came the big day I saw my Mom and Dad argue for the first time. I remember the day like it was yesterday. It was the first time I ever heard my mother be cross with my Dad. It was Friday and Dad was half an hour late coming home from work. I heard the disagreement from in the house. I was seven years old and went outside to investigate. My mom saw me coming and said the last word of their argument. I heard her say: "The dang thing even has a hole in it and you bought it anyway!" She turned around and went in the house.

As I got closer I saw the thing my parents were discussing. Dad had traded his small boat and some cash to a guy in Genoa for a bigger boat. Dad lifted me up and put me in behind the wheel. This boat was weird. It had a steering wheel halfway to the front. I was used to watching Dad run the boat from the rear. Dad explained to me that steering wheels were the wave of the future and every boat would have them in ten years. I asked Dad about the hole Mom was talking about. I remember exactly what he said: "That little hole can be fixed easily and you won't even know there was a hole there after I am done fixing it."

The next day was Saturday and Dad was already out there trying to fix that hole. His new boat attracted some of the neighbors. They all complimented him on his new boat with the steering wheel as they looked at it. They were all very obviously jealous. By the end of the day there were four guys "helping" Dad fix the hole. They were working at it even after dark because it was late fall and he wanted to get it out on the water before winter.

On Sunday Dad and two of his friends loaded up and went to the Mississippi to christen the boat. I heard them picking on him before they left and calling him "Captain" Harris. One hour after they left, the boat and vehicle pulled back up in front of the house. The patch job did not hold. Dad's friends were razzing him and told him that he as the "captain" should have gone down with the ship.

The captain did not get the boat back on the water that fall and it was covered and parked in the yard for the winter. Mom pestered Dad all winter and tried to get him to sell it. He told her that the boat would more than pay for itself with fish he was going to provide for the family in that boat. Dad had the boat ready in the spring and he took me and my oldest sister out instead of his friends that had picked on him. This time the patch held.

The Kickapoo River was so close he took up bank pole fishing for catfish. We went daily down the "Kick" to pull in massive catfish. I still remember the smell of rotten chicken liver. That was our prime bait for cats.

It was May of 1965 when it happened. Dad let me steer the boat all by myself on the Mississippi. He was going back to a hidden slough and the water was shallower than he thought and he got stuck. He took the oar and was poling us through the mud. I got to steer and it made me feel like I was the king of the world. I ran from the car at the end of the day and went in the house and told all my sisters about steering the boat. Mom chastised Dad at first for letting an eight year old steer a boat. Dad told Mom about the mud and they both thought 12 years old was a proper age for me to be able to operate the boat.

The days on the water were excellent. Almost every week Dad bought something new for the boat or a new fishing pole. Mom was really losing patience with Dad for spending so much money on his hobbies. He told her that the rod and reel he had just purchased was only 45 dollars. I thought it was odd that he said that he said that because I was there when he bought the combo and it was 90 dollars. Dad and I had a talk about fishing gear and women later. He told me that sometimes the prices of things had to be fudged so Mom would not get so mad at him for buying them. He swore me to secrecy on the real prices of all fishing and hunting gear I witnessed being purchased.

Our life fishing was grand. Dad told tales to all the neighbors about our catches. We supplied the town with catfish and walleye on a regular basis. There was even a sign-up sheet at the gas station in town for Len Harris' catfish or walleyes.

This all changed in November of 1967. Dad went to northern Wisconsin to deer hunt with his brother and never came back to captain the boat again. Dad died of a heart attack. He left behind six children and a wife that had never worked out of the home.

Two days after the funeral it started. Guys that Dad had fished with or hunted with showed up at the door to "help" my mother. It got out that Dad didn't have life insurance and Mom was strapped for cash. Dad's guns were the first casualties. I remember one guy offering Mom 35 bucks for his rod and reel he had paid 90 dollars for. I wanted to say something but thought better of it and shut my mouth.

The next spring there was a guy in our yard looking at Dad's boat. I heard him offer her 300 dollars for it. She said she would think on it and get back with him. I told my Uncle Sig about the dilemma and what Dad had told me the boat had really cost and Sig told Mom to not take a penny under 600 dollars for it. There were many tire kickers that year. Mom fielded many offers for the boat. None even came close to 600 dollars. I was relieved every time someone left and the boat was still in the yard. I was eleven years old and I got it into my head that when I turned twelve the next June the boat would be mine because Mom and Dad had already talked about it and that was the age I could steer the boat myself.

My birthday came and I was twelve in 1969. I went out in the yard and took the cover off the boat. I sat behind the steering wheel and remembered all the good times I had spent with Dad in that very special boat. I cleaned it out and prepared it for going on the Kickapoo. Dad taught me how to make those bank poles for catfish. I thought that was close and I should go and cut down some saplings and make some bank poles and set up the rigs just like he had taught me. I had the poles all made up. All I needed was chicken liver. I checked the couch cushions and there was enough change for them. Off I went to the grocery store.

My twelve year old mind was abuzz. I left the store and was walking home. I was planning where I was going to put all the bank poles. I saw a car coming down Main Street and it had a boat behind it. I would always look at boats and compare them to my Dad's with the fancy steering wheel and gloat that ours was better. The boat behind the car looked a lot like "mine." I thought to myself that it wasn't as good as mine because it didn't have a steering wheel. As the car went by I saw this one had a steering wheel and a repaired front. I ran home as fast as I could to tell Mom that someone had stolen the boat. Mom was outside. I yelled at her to call the police because someone had stolen my boat. Mom's eyes got really big and she shook her head and looked down. An hour later and lots of crying by me it sunk in that Mom had sold the boat for 800 dollars. She explained to me that our family was having a hard time making ends meet and the guy had seen me playing in the boat and was attracted to it and saw the "For Sale" sign. As a twelve year old I didn't understand very well. It took me until about the age of 18 to realize that mom did what she had to do.

I have never owned a boat in my life and never will.

THE NINE-YEAR-OLD
TROUT MASTER

I t was September of 2010. I was driving home from a trout outing and saw him. He was hopping over a barb wire fence out in the middle of nowhere. The area he came out of was buck brush central. It was so tight in there I bet he had to walk backwards in some places to get through, even though he couldn't have been more than nine years old. I slowed down alongside of him. I rolled down the window and asked him if everything was okay. He flashed a huge smile at me and said: "Better than alright." He bent over and picked up his Zebco 404 with one hand and his stringer with the other. The stringer had two massive brown trout hanging on it. I let out an audible "WOW!" when I saw the stringer.

The kid gave me the short version of his exploits. He told me he recognized me from me doing a trout presentation at his school the year prior. The young trout master introduced himself as Michael. Michael was way out in the sticks and there was no farm anywhere near so I offered him a ride home. He accepted the ride because he was way tired and he remembered me from when I visited his school.

On the way to his house he told me that he only went on this stretch three to four times a year and always did well. I told him I had also fished today and my results were nowhere near as good as his. The trip went by quickly and we pulled into Michael's driveway. Michael introduced to his Dad. He had told his Dad about me after I spoke at his school. Two hours later and about thirty trout stories swapped between us I drove away. Michael had invited me to fish with him and we had set the date for two days later. Michael's family owned the three farm stretch and I received permission to fish it any time I wanted.

Michael's Dad dropped us off at the starting point of our fish and I parked at the top or ending place. Dad drove away and wished us luck. Four hours later and only one fish in my creel we got to the truck. Michael had caught three really nice browns. The smallest was eighteen inches. Michael and I talked on the way back to his house. He told me his grandpa had taught him all the good places on the stretch and that was why I did so poorly because he had "home field advantage." Those were his words. I had paid attention to where Michael had caught the trout but not really close attention. The weeds and brush were really thick on the stretch and it was a long and tiring outing.

Michael and I went out two more times before the end of the year to fish. Each time out Michael kicked trout tail and he caught two or three monsters when I caught maybe one. I was not a quitter so I fished the stretch five more times before the end of September and season closed. I got skunked all five times. The stretch of water was unclassified water. The nearest classified trout water was four miles upstream.

March came and I wanted to go fishing with Michael again. Michael said he did not go fishing during catch and release season because his grandpa had taught him that injuring trout for sport alone was unethical. I went on my own and was skunked again. I stopped by at Michael's house and told him of my lack of success. He told me to come back the next day and he would go along with no pole and give me some pointers. I smiled inside when he said that and thought, "What the heck, there might be something I am missing on stream. Maybe he can give me a tip or two."

I picked him up the next morning and off we went. I had brought an extra pole along to try to talk him into fishing. He was adamant about his stance on injuring trout for sport and declined the offer to use my extra rod. Four hours later and me releasing a dozen trout over 17 inches, we were finished. He had pointed out every place to cast. I asked him on each specific place why there? I wanted to get some insight on the reasons. Each time Michael told me that is where grandpa had told him to cast. Michael did not know the rhyme or reason for the areas to cast. He just remembers that was where his grandpa had told him to cast. Grandpa was fishing in heaven so I couldn't ask him.

It was March and the weeds were all down. The stream looked much different than it did in September. Each place I caught a decent fish had a common theme. There were swamps or small springs in the area. The swamps didn't empty into the waterway so I was a little puzzled. I took the water temperatures downstream of the swamps and there was a dramatic difference in temperatures. These swamps leeched into the stream by being in close proximity through the ground. There was no obvious entry point into the waterway. The springs emptying in were obvious now because the weeds were down and I could see them entering. The mystery was solved!

Trout are very temperature dependent. The outside weather directly affects the stream temperatures. In the middle of summer there can be four to eight degree temperature difference in the water due to swamps or springs leeching in to the water. Most swamps are caused by springs. Ground water comes out at about 42 degrees. That swamp leeching in the stream can have a dramatic effect on fishing. Warmer water holds less dissolved oxygen. Those swamps and small trickles that you can only see when the weeds are down are the keys. The same goes for cold weather conditions. A March day the water temps can be near the freezing point. Those thermals "swamps and small springs" can raise the water temps four to eight degrees and that rise in temperature can turn on a lethargic trout that is unwilling to move due to cold water.

One time about fifteen years ago I was a member of a shocking crew. They went out on a July day when the outdoor temps were in the low 90s. Most of the stream temps were in the middle 70s and dangerous for the fish to be caught in. The shocking crew leader showed me the "thermal" effects, and got excited about 100 yards before each. He told me the trout would literally stick their noses into the banks where swamps leeched in and at the tiny springs that fed into the waterway. That marginal water you drive by or scoff at as frog water might have thermals. Bigger trout can tolerate warmer water. Most of these places are quality water, not quantity.

Keep your eyes open the next time you are fishing. Look for thermals. A decent thermometer is needed. Every once in awhile take the temperature where you caught a fish and you will be amazed at the difference. The area might have an underwater spring feeding in. Most of all keep an open mind and let a nine your old trout master help you if he offers.

THE SURE THING

My friend from Pennsylvania was visiting Wisconsin. He told me he had a morning to do some running and gunning. He just wanted to catch a couple fish and be on his way back to Pennsylvania. He wanted easy access and a nice place to fish. He was a little bit of a "doubting Thomas" when I showed him the run. He strung up his three weight rod the way I explained. Again he thought me to be a bit crazy. I explained to him that he should fish a size ten turkey leech through there with an indicator. He refused the indicator and threw the leech in the hole thirty times and wanted to move on. He also had a 5X leader on and I asked him to size up to a 4X minimum. He was set in his ways and said he could handle any fish with 5X on his 3 weight. He said it was a worthless hole and he didn't get a single bite in the hole.

I told him that I had seen a video once that proved to me that fly anglers miss 40 percent of their hits because of the lack of an indicator. After a little of coaxing he put on a "bobber." He was old school and anything that looked like fishing with bait was against his belief system.

I explained to him that my father had showed me this hole as a small child and he always used a piece of cork on the line here on his fly rod with a crawler and ALWAYS kicked trout tail. The trout stacked up just below the step drop. There were always big fish at the top and small tail end Charlies at the back. That was the pecking order. They line up just like they were waiting to go to a movie.

Many years of fishing the area had taught me the lay of this hole. If I fished a hole hard and believed I was not going to catch another fish in a hole, I would walk into the hole to map the bottom for a return trip.

That mapping told me that the corner directly above this hole swung the current into the bank and eroded the bank under that tree and there was a serious step drop there. The alpha trout typically has the top of the hole at the tight step drop. It has the bank to break the current and is in the best feeding lay. The current also magnified the size of fish in the hole and under gunned anglers usually left with their tail between their legs.

My buddy "Mark" swung "my" fly I gave him tight to the right bank about fifteen feet above the hole. I was getting preachy and told him to keep it tight to the right bank because the alpha trout would be there. He gave me this blank stare and said something again about this being a worthless hole.

Then it happened. He wasn't even paying attention to the indicator and I screamed, "BITE!!!! BITE!!!" Mark's reactions were slow but he did have a hook up for about a half a second and broke off his 5X leader. We got to see the 18-20 inch brown at the surface and Mark was sick because it broke off. I explained to him the current magnification I told him about prior. The current was fast in the hole and told him he needed to keep his line short or he would miss bites with a big belly in the line. He started listening to every word I said then.

Five minutes later and a 4X leader on he wanted to throw back in there right away. I told him to let the run calm down. That big fish flashing on its side when it was hooked surely alerted any smart fish in the hole and it was best to wait. We actually sat down and talked about the hole.

I explained the bottom to him. He was very attentive now. He wanted to know how I knew exactly how the bottom laid. I explained to him my after-fishing mapping trick. This was an unusual hole. The water was shallow upstream and there was an obvious bend that shot the spring floods into the bank directly above the tree on the right. The tree roots kept the bank solid so the water bounced back out. I pointed at the bottom above the hole. The bottom was rocky and not silty so I told him more than likely the hole was that way too. That spring flooding also had a bounce back to it.

He wanted to know what a bounce back was. The current slamming into the hard bank with the tree roots stabilizing it caused a bounce back effect, and the beginning of the hole was much farther out from the bank than one would think. There was almost a wing dam there because of the bounce back. I showed him the color difference in the hole and he could imagine the wing dam effect from the water color. This step drop ran a good eight feet from the bank out into the main channel and the current going under the tree also ripped out a good place.

Three hours later and twenty trout from the same hole, Mark was sold on strike indicators. He broke off one other large fish that took him into the roots and his three weight didn't have enough backbone to turn the fish out of them. We talked about that tree eventually falling in the water from the floods. I explained to him that that little tree was at least 20 years old and Mother Nature is better at making trout streams then any back hoe or pallet maker.

Mark questioned me if maybe we were directly behind the stocking truck because of his outstanding luck. His smile was huge when I told him the fish manager from that stream did not stock fish. Mark left to PA after just one hole. Don't let prejudice or nonsensical unwritten rules ruin your trout outing. A sure thing can come with worms, flies and spinners.

The really sad part of this story is the landowner sold the rights to the WDNR and they manicured the area and that tree was one of the first things they took out. The hole is utterly worthless now.

THE TACKLE BOX

I ran into Scot Schellhorn on Friday at the Apple Festival in Gays Mills. Scot and I usually talk fishing when we meet. This was one of those talks. Scot was a little more excited than typical. He had inherited his Dad's tackle box. He wanted me to look at it. I will quote Scot: "There are some really old neat lures in there of my Dad's and he thought he might sell them if I thought they were worth anything." I told him I would make time and come to his house and take a look.

Sunday morning I drove into his driveway and found him splitting wood outside. He knew what I was there for and he almost jogged up his driveway to the garage to retrieve "the tackle box." He walked out of the garage cradling it in his arms like a baby. It had a handle but Scot carried it with both arms clutching it close to his chest. From that second on I knew Scot really didn't want to sell any of those lures. He just wanted to show me that special tackle box.

Scot opened it carefully and I could feel his excitement as he did it. He quickly found his favorite lure. He held it up like a prize and said: "This was my favorite lure. I could catch any kind of fish in any waterway with this one!"

He went back to the corner of the garage and retrieved the creel and the "helicopter" lures. These were our big fish catchers. I could see the twinkle in Scot's eyes as he touched each one of the lures and described them. At one time I could see Scot's mind wander to a long ago memory. The twinkle in his eyes told me he was with his Dad in Hudson, Iowa fishing and he was ten years old again.

There was one special lure that had glass eyes and he had to show it to me. He made me look closely at the lure to show me a tooth mark on it. He said he didn't get to see that fish but it almost ripped the rod out of his hand. He could still remember the disappointment he felt from not landing that fish. He was just a little tike and his Dad reassured him there would be many big fish in his future.

That tackle box seemed to have an endless supply of lures and reels and many memories in it. The "rocket" reel still was in its box and the price tag and manual were in there. It cost $13.95. Scot commented that some good line costs more than that today. Scot's eyebrows raised as he showed me one special reel and his eyes got big. Scot exclaimed: "The Rocket was for bass and huge catfish!"

Scot was truly caught up in the moment. He was showing me all the treasures his Dad's tackle box held. The Martin reel held many memories of days past. When we were done and I had taken some photos, I told Scot he was a lucky man to inherit such a tackle box, and that if I owned it and it was my Dad's there would be zero chances of me selling anything in that box. Scot smiled widely. I watched as he put everything back in the tackle box. He was very meticulous as he did it. He wanted to make sure it was all put back in there correctly just like his Dad had taught him. There is ZERO chance that Scot will ever sell anything from this time capsule of his days fishing with his Dad. I checked back with Scot and told him I was going to include this story in my book. Scot smiled and said: "My dad would really like that."

I submitted this story to the Hudson, Iowa newspaper. This is Scott's hometown. The editor knew Scott's family well and used the story in the paper. I was contacted by many of Scott's relatives and thanked for running the story for them to read and to cherish.

THE WIND CHIMES

I purchased two nice wind chimes this spring for the deck. Neither my wife nor daughter was a fan of them. The first two weeks they were out there my daughter went out in the middle of the night and took them down because she couldn't sleep with them going outside her window.

My sister Deb suggested I ask our mother if she wanted the chimes. I visit my elderly mother on Wednesdays every week. I told her about the dilemma. She volunteered to take both of them off my hands. I took both of them to her yesterday.

We talked for a while and I learned from her that my father loved wind chimes. I didn't know this fact. It didn't surprise me because Dad was a nature guy and he considered wind chimes an extension of the outdoors.

Mom picked the one she liked and told me the other one my Dad would like and I should take them to him. I thought this was an odd request because he had passed away in 1967. She told me there was a metal stand with a hook on the gravesite and the wind chimes would look and sound beautiful there.

Through the years I have visited his grave typically a couple days before Memorial Day. My Dad has a purple lilac bush on his grave and it was in full bloom. It was his request to have such a bush on his grave.

My wife and I put the wind chime up last night. It began to sound immediately. The strange thing is, there was no wind. This really freaked me out. Ever since I have been little it has spooked me to visit my Dad's grave. Something about seeing your own name on a grave stone has always bothered me. I am a junior.

We stood there and listened to the chimes toll and smelled the lilacs for quite a while. My mind was racing. I have never been comfortable being in the cemetery ever. The sound and smell made me linger there and think.

I dropped off my wife at her mother's and went to the dam in Gays Mills to fish. I stood there a while before I fished and pondered. Many a day in my youth I had sat on the banks of the Kickapoo River and fished with my father. I was the happiest as a kid when I was out in nature with my Dad.

The cemetery was about two miles away but I swear I could hear those wind chimes singing. It finally came to me why I am so driven to fish. I wanted to be with my Dad. He was taken from me when I was ten years old. Being on stream was like being with him. Every change of the wind was like he was speaking to me. I could see his smile as I landed a big trout or pike. He never really died. He is part of the outdoors. This was the real reason I escaped into the outdoors every chance I could throughout my life. His body was at the cemetery but his spirit was with me on stream and he had never left.

MY BOOK OF LIFE

Yesterday I fished alone on a long wooded stretch. I typically don't like fishing alone. If I have a fishing partner I have someone to talk to and a photo subject. Yesterday was different. I went alone to have some "me" time. Some recent news had me thinking about why I fish.

I started on my fishing journey at age five. I am fifty-seven now. My first outing is very vivid in my mind to this day. My recent outings have been a little labored due to my back problems. They are shorter outings and I have lost my path a little. My focus seems clouded and not about the big picture.

Yesterday when I fished I was thinking about my past and what led me to this journey that is trout fishing. It was easy to establish my starting point and my motives. The big trout bug bit me on my very first outing at age five.

The other anglers that have taken a similar journey talk about the evolution of a trout angler. I was always of the opinion that I was stuck on that big trout level and that was why I fished. Yesterday as I fished I did some soul searching. The reason I trout fish came to me and it wasn't just one thing or the next big trout.

I take lots of photos when I am out on stream. Every so often I get a photo or two taken of me holding a trout. Every person that has ever taken a photo of me asks me why I don't smile when I am holding a big trout? I thought about it yesterday.

What makes me smile when I am out there? I caught myself smiling a lot when wandering yesterday. It clicked and it was a self aware moment. I thought back in to my book of life and it was obvious.

Early season trout fishing is cold and stark. The snow is typically deep and I wear out easier. The environment is not inviting like the lush greens of summer, but there is an allure to those days of frozen guides and numb fingers. The long winter has made me forget the gnats and mosquitoes of late September. My heart yearns to brave the crisp days of Wisconsin's early season.

I like to be the first one to place a footstep in fresh snow of opening morning. It makes me feel like I am the first angler to ever set foot on that stream. One of my biggest smiles I can ever remember fishing is when the snow was coming down hard on one of those frigid openers. The snow was going down the back of my coat and then that big broad smile was painted on my face. You would have had to experience it yourself to feel what it meant to me. The solitude was deafening.

Spring comes quickly to my home waters. I don't miss a beat and am out there fishing and continuing my journey. The smells are amazing in spring. The ground melting has a unique smell to it. The trees are budding and the grasp of winter is being shed. The world is becoming anew. That very first smell of a plum tree blooming triggers a smile for me. The smell is better than any expensive perfume from Paris or New York. I feel alive again and I am anew.

Early summer comes and with it the baby birds and the sounds of the stream come with them. The first wildflowers appear. Not far after that the wood anemones and blue bells paint a tapestry on the valley floors. My stream is a veritable sensory smorgasbord. A constant smile is painted on my face. My stream is alive and me with it.

Summer brings hot and biting insects. My lust for the stream is dampened by the stifling hot, but I trudge on. What more could an angler wish for? I am one of those crazy guys that wade in water and mud up to their belly buttons and enjoy it. The only thing that could make it better would be a slow steady rain. Are you smiling now?

September comes quickly. The trees begin to change color. The leaves on your sentinels of the streams are tipped with gold. You need to layer up to fish because that cold wind has whispered to you that winter will come quickly. If you are not smiling now, then you need to lay your pole down and take up golf.

My very good friend was diagnosed with liver and colon cancer this spring. He is upbeat and positive. I was bashful at first to talk to him about it. It made me feel so mortal and close to death myself. We talked this weekend. He was candid about his condition. His positive thought process was obvious. I noticed he smiled a lot during our conversation. I need to learn to smile more often.

HINDSIGHT

The classic line by Thoreau: "Many men go *fishing all of their lives* without knowing that it is *not fish they are after*" has never struck home so intensely than it has for me as of late. I will admit that at times in my life I have taken my love for the outdoors and fishing for granted. I look back at days of old and think about the hindsight is 20/20 adage.

December 3rd, 2013, I had fusion on vertebrae L4 and L5 to correct problems with my thighs falling asleep when I stood too long. I have been dealing with this problem for about five years. I put off back surgery because of the unknown it carried. I could be fixed or I could incur a domino effect in other vertebrae in my back and have many more problems.

Tuesday January 28th I go back to the same hospital that I had back surgery to see a knee specialist. I am looking at complete left knee replacement. I am also having my back above my fusion site looked at due to excruciating pain in my middle back. Knee replacement could require six months of rehab. This would completely make my trout season for 2014 a wash.

A dozen years ago I gave up deer hunting because my wife and daughter refused to eat venison. They will eat trout if I smoke it. As a teenager I fished and hunted anything that swam, flew or walked. I voluntarily gave up some outdoor pursuits but I had never been forced to before. This feeling is not something that any avid trout angler wants to see or hear. There is a definite feeling of helplessness going on for me.

I plan on recuperating and being back out there in late 2014 or opener 2015. I can't help it to say that I have thought about what if I can't go back out there and beat the bushes for trout like I love so dearly. These feelings are intense and depress me. I was sitting looking out the window tonight at the snow and the tree bending in the breeze and I was trying to think what I would miss the most if I couldn't regain my health and go fishing again. What would I miss the most?

About a week ago I made comment to an acquaintance about trout fishing being so important to me and he dismissed it. He said trout fishing was the least important thing he does in life and I shouldn't make it so important. I wholeheartedly disagree with him.

Many people go to church to feel spiritual and be in touch with the universe. I go into the outdoors to cleanse my soul. All the things in life that bother me are melted away about a hundred yards from the truck. The fish are only a bonus in the whole scheme of things.

The question has been nagging me. What would I miss the most? I wrote a list of things that I found in my log books of 27 years that jumped out at me. Some things on the list were just childhood memories. The list was really long and there was only one fish involved. There were things written in my logs that happened almost every year. Here are my top ten:

1. The rush of the unknown potential of what lays beneath the water on every cast.
2. The feeling of a crisp spring breeze on my cheek.
3. Wildflowers on stream.
4. The sounds of the wind and the water.
5. The smell of the first plum blossoms.
6. The way the sun glistens off the water.
7. The feeling of being the first person on that particular stream that season.
8. My first trout outing in the rain.
9. Fishing in the snow.
10. Missing fishing during the closed season.

What will I do if I am unable to return to the stream? Is there some other kind of hobby that could replace what I do in the outdoors? I have thought about getting a boat and being a little more passive of an angler. This doesn't seem like an even trade. Every deer season that opens I miss hunting. I am even more into trout fishing and I don't think it can be replaced. In the captain story earlier in the book I said I would never get a boat. A new chapter in my life is about to be written. My father loved boats and I see a boat in my near future.

TROUT FISHING IN GERMANY

I lived in Germany from 1978 to 1984. The trout fishing there is legendary. The glacier fed streams were cold to say the least. While in the Army there I decided it was much too rich for my blood. I was an Army Sergeant there.

Fishing in Germany was quite an undertaking. There were classes to get a license that cost nearly a thousand dollars and after you took your "hard" test you had to rent the waterway you planned to fish. When you fished the waterway, you had to rent it from the individual or club that owns the rights for the waterway. Also you had to present the trout to the land owner and if he wanted it you must give it up. No matter if it was a trophy or a dink. My limited army income made it nearly impossible.

While in the service, I made numerous friends with the locals. My best friend in Germany is called Jan Tomasak. I met him the first day I arrived in country. I flagged him down. He was taxi driver. He was a college student working his way through Architecture School. I asked him to show me around the city. Jan turned off his taxi meter and went off duty. Jan showed me through every nook and cranny of Augsburg. This boy knew Augsburg. We became best friends. The years passed and the women passed but one thing stayed the same. Jan was my best friend and would be for life.

Jan had dreams of big things. He talked about retiring at age 40. He had the drive and I thought it could be possible. I departed Augsburg Germany in 1984. Jan had his first architecture business already started.

Five years after I returned to the USA I invited Jan to Wisconsin to be my photographer for my wedding. He jumped at the opportunity. He stayed at my mother's house in Gays Mills. He was quite a hit with the locals.

It was my wedding day and Jan was down in the basement of the church with me. We were standing at the back door of the church in the basement. He opened the door and told me: "This is your last chance to escape." I just smiled and told him: "No way." His response was: "Good, I would have tripped you and carried you inside if you did something so foolish. This one is a keeper."

Jan flew back to Germany that next day. We went to visit him a couple times in the '90s. He was becoming quite the business man. His business was flourishing. He even talked about expanding to East Germany when it opened. The East opened. Jan was The Man. He went into the old country and made some good business investments. He sold all his holdings and bought twelve apartment buildings in Augsburg. That same year he invited my family to the Millennium Ball he was throwing in the Czech Republic. It was a black tie affair with all guests being transported to the Castle in the Alps by a eight white stallion carriage. Evening gowns were a requirement. It was too rich for my blood but I was really impressed by Jan's success.

Five years passed and I had to listen to Jan saying he was retiring that year at age 40 and we needed to come visit him. He wanted me to go trout fishing with him. He was a member of the Munich Fishing Club. They owned all the rights to southern Germany for trout fishing. I was to be his guest with no fees or school required. The Guest Pass needed to be carried with us.

July 2005 Barb and I went to Germany. I was planning the trip for six months prior. One month before we went I sent a big package over with backup fish clothing and all sorts of gear. I had it planned down to the last detail. I was going to spank some German trout tail.

Barb and I arrived in Munich on a Thursday morning. The fight was non-stop and I tried to sleep on the plane. I was too excited. I could not sleep. I drove from Munich to Oberau in a rent a car. I was spent. I needed to sleep. We checked in to the Edelweiss Hotel at eleven a.m. Barb and I were fast asleep.

Two hours later there was a knock at the door. We rolled over and ignored it. The knock was louder the next time and lots longer. I answered the door. It was Jan. He wanted to go fishing. I told him I was beat and needed to sleep a while. He was insistent and said he wanted to just drive around and talk about fishing and do a little scouting.

Jan explained to me that we were going to fish in the Leinbach River and it was a ten minute drive from my hotel. I thought what the heck. There was nothing wrong with scouting. As we drove he told me the German Fishing Regulations. Between the two of us we had a one day pass and we could catch one meter of trout and then we had to quit. The Munich club had a strict "NO CATCH AND RELEASE" policy. Anything we caught no matter the size had to be kept.

We got out of his van stream side and he started gearing up. I told him this was only a scouting mission. I needed to sleep. He told me: "You can sleep when you are dead....We are fishing." I protested. I told him I needed to get my gear out and waders and boxes. He handed me the rod he had already strung up with a Mepps oddball looking spinner I had never seen before and said, "It is time to fish."

He told me the trout were hard to catch and don't feel bad if we didn't catch anything. I took my wallet out of my blue jeans and took everything out of my pockets and off we went. The streams were tiny. The only place they widened was where the glaciers emptied in. I tried casting from shore but I couldn't reach where I wanted. My wife Barb got bored with watching us fishing and went wandering. I waded right in to the stream up to my waist. The streams were ultra cold. After the shock of the water and some serious shrinkage I placed myself in a good casting position.

Twenty minutes later I had THREE 15 inch trout and I was done fishing. All the months of preparation and shipping of gear were over in twenty minutes. Jan just smiled and said: "More time to go to local beer fests and enjoy the sights." We went to my friend's home in Oberau and cleaned the three browns and cooked them on the grill. It was an excellent trip to Germany. My friend Jan and I still contact each other about once a month. He is retired and travels all over the world. He bought a place in Bratislava and I have an open invitation to fish with him. It may happen someday but I am not shipping anything over ahead of time.

PERSPECTIVE

L ast spring the phone rang and it was my old friend Jim. We talked for quite some time. He shared with me that one of his sons had recently broken up with his wife of ten years and wasn't doing well. He asked me if I would take Brad fishing and take his mind off his dilemma. I had fished with Brad a dozen times in the past and enjoyed his company and thought it would be a good idea to get him out in nature and get his mind off his worries. I knew the exact place to take him.

We met up on the outskirts of town. We talked a little and off we went to our destination with two cars. We parked Brad's truck at the upper part of where we were to fish and Brad jumped in with me and we drove down to the lower beginning area. Brad was really quiet and I did not pry. I thought if he wanted to talk about it he would.

I had not fished this stretch in early season before. The stream looked very different than it had in the green of summer. The bluffs and landscape seemed a little more stark and not so lush and beautiful. The beginning stretch was cradled by rock bluffs. I let Brad fish a little ahead of me so he could get the rust off his casting and catch his first fish. It didn't take long and Brad had a beautiful brook trout to hand. The colors of the trout were neon and seemed out of place with the browns of early spring. We admired the male brook trout and sent it back to its home.

I then decided to fish alongside Brad so we could talk. He opened up and told me his wife had left him out of the blue and told him he should take the two boys because she wanted to start a new life. He was having a hard time with the transition and his five year old and seven year old boys didn't understand the situation at all. I could see he just wanted to fish and leave his problems behind for the day. We continued on with our adventure.

Brad really liked the rock bluffs. He said they made him feel safe and looked after. The water was crystal clear and the trout were eager. I watched Brad catch a decent brown and he admired it and *set it free*. Brad stayed crouched for a while after the release and I walked up to him. He wiped tears away and stood up and continued to fish.

The next hole looked perfect. The weeds that were typically there had died off from the cold winter weather. We could see activity at the head of the hole. Brad stood in one place and caught twenty trout. Each one of his casts seemed easier and smoother. The soothing effect of nature and the trout melted away his anguish.

The brown of early spring were the dominant colors when we began our adventure. As we went upstream the color began to change to a little more green. I explained to Brad that there were lots of springs in the area and that was why the color was changing. Brad just nodded his head and did not speak. It was obvious he was still quite injured by his wife. We slowly fished upstream. The only words exchanged were when we admired a trout we had caught.

We walked up on to the biggest hole on the stretch. I told Brad it was his to fish. I sat down and watched as Brad dissected the hole. Brad fished there for 45 minutes. He changed flies ten times and sized down his tippet with no results. Brad and I talked about the hole and where the trout would be laying. Brad said he felt defeated by the hole. I quickly told him that maybe there was only one really big trout in the hole and we had not thrown something it wanted to eat. I smiled and said maybe next time you will catch the monster that lives there.

Brad wanted to know how I stayed positive throughout my life. Brad had read many of my stories about my youth. He wanted to hear how I kept upbeat when my Dad died when I was 10 years old and left my mother and five sisters behind. I told Brad my mother had always stayed positive. She had always shared with us stories about other families that were worse off than we were.

Brad was through with the hole so I went to the head of it to take a photo. I snapped a photo and I saw something in the foreground. There were a couple structures about 30 yards from the stream. I had never seen these structures before because I had always fished this area in summer and now the vegetation was down and I could see well. Brad and I went to investigate.

The first structure was round and at first glance looked like an outhouse. It was made of stone blocks and the door opened only partially down. The roof was made of stones and there was an opening in the middle. The roof was moss covered. I kidded Brad that the moss was probably older than he was. We decided it was an old smokehouse. It seemed way out of place out there in the boonies with no roads and limited access. A smokehouse was a necessity not a luxury back in the day to make it through harsh Wisconsin weather. They smoked the fish and game the family gathered and preserved it for the long frigid Wisconsin winters.

We went to the next structure. It was about thirty yards away and tucked up against the hill. We both walked up to it and had the same comment. We both said "WOW!" simultaneously.

There we stood in front of an open hearth and chimney. There was no house attached to the structure. The family that had lived there was long gone. We admired the stone work. I told Brad I bet that the whole family helped make that hearth and that many meals were shared in the glow of the fire it created. I could almost smell the wood burning. I visualized the large black cast iron pot hanging over the flames. For a moment I was teleported back in time in front of that raging hearth and I could smell a hearty meal being prepared. We guessed the home to be 80 - 100 years old.

Where had the family gone? Did a fire take their home? Did the Spanish influenza epidemic of 1918 destroy their family like it did many families in Wisconsin? Had the Wisconsin winters been just too harsh for the family to withstand? It seemed like an amazing homestead site with the stream so close for bathing, water and food. This place must have seemed perfect when the home was built up against the hill sheltered by the rock bluffs.

The sun was going down fast and we needed to keep fishing. Brad seemed like a different man. He had more energy in his casts and a smile on his face. The two hours of fishing just flew by. We were at Brad's truck in what seemed like a blink of an eye. We stuck our rods in his truck and headed to my truck. We stood in the waning light of the day and took our waders off and talked. Brad thanked me for taking him and said it was fate that we stumbled on that old homestead. His life was easy and the family that had once lived in that old homestead had put his life in perspective. He drove away with a big smile.

I lingered before I left and took in all of nature's beauty. I do this each time I go out. I believe you are defined by your journey through life. Be the driver during that journey and not always the passenger.

PS: Brad's Dad contacted me last week and he told that Brad got married again and the smile on his face is back.

RODNEY

R od and I have been good friends since I was fourteen years old. His family took me deer hunting many times when I was young. The whole Johnson Clan is very warmhearted and a generous bunch. The first time I met Rod was on the Main Street of Gays Mills. He was roaring up and down the street with his new Charger RT. I flagged down Rod and made some small talk. I had something I wanted him to do for me. I knew he was 18 years old and I wanted him to carry out for me. He agreed and I handed him the money. I told him a six pack of Blue Ribbon is what I wanted. He smiled and asked me what I was going to drink? His payment was beer for carrying out and I needed to double my amount I gave him so we could have a 12 pack. He went right in the bar and picked up the beer and off we drove in his race car. We have made many adventures through the years. Rod was even one of my groomsmen in my wedding.

Last year Rod was diagnosed with colon and liver cancer. The prognosis was not very good. Rod and his wife Karen stayed positive and Rod started chemotherapy earlier this year. The bills were racking up for the cancer treatment so there was a benefit for Rod at the Gays Mills Community Center. Rod looked skinny and his color was not very good. He is a fighter and it was obvious he and his family were doing all they could do to battle his cancer. There was an overwhelming turn out for the benefit. Over double the number of people that the family projected for attendance came to support Rod and Karen.

About a month ago Rod had a portion of his colon removed. They believe they got the cancer in his colon but, the cancer in the liver was still present. The doctors are going to aggressively attack the cancer in Rod's liver next week.

I ran into Rod last Friday night. He was at his traditional night before Deer Hunting gathering at the local pub. Since his surgery he gained back 10 pounds and his color returned to normal. He seemed like the same old Rodney. He told me about some type of aggressive chemo wash he was going to get the next week. He showed me the direct line that the doctors had placed in his chest for chemotherapy. He was very upbeat and announced he was going hunting opening day.

Rod showed me his special permit for hunting. Wisconsin allows seriously sick hunters to hunt from their vehicles. Rod was really pumped up about going hunting. He told me he would be satisfied with even a little doe. He was just happy that he could deer hunt with his illness. We sat and talked for over three hours about the old days and hunts past. When I left I told him that he was going to get a big buck and no small doe.

Rod parked his truck out in the pasture behind the family farm opening day. Right after first light Rod harvested this massive buck. Having cancer is very scary but if you fight it and be positive you can beat it. Rod, you have many more deer hunting years in your future.

UNPREPARED

The trout season of 2013 was a major bust for me due to lack of mobility. I had my worst big trout year of my life. I attributed it to my bad left knee and back. I decided that 2014 was not going to be that way. I pestered my doctor and had back fusion surgery done on December 3, 2013. I also have left knee surgery scheduled in early 2014. I want to be ready for 2014 trout.

Late December came and my back was feeling better and I had the itch to fish. My wife Barb tried to dissuade me from going down to the dam in Gays Mills. She told me the snow was too deep and I might hurt my back or knee. Me being the pigheaded person I am I did not listen. Off we went to Gays Mills.

We parked at the west side of the river by the wall side. The wall stood about four and a half feet above the water and had some benches to sit on. The only problems were that no one had been down there for two months and the benches had snow on them and the wall was covered with fourteen inches of snow.

My wife Barb went down the steep hill first and blazed a trail with the gear. She leaned the rod against the bench and went back and retrieved the ultra long handled net and placed it where I instructed her to. She then went up the bank and slowly walked down the bank with me behind her. She thought if I fell she could at least catch me before I ended up in the water.

We made it down the bank safe and sound. She had stomped down the snow so I had a good casting area. I hooked on my silver little cleo and assessed the situation. The year before I had a behemoth pike cruising through the carp that school there make an appearance for me with a small carp in its mouth. The memory was quite fresh in my mind. The carp were schooled there just like the year before. I smiled and let my first cast fly. No takers on first and second cast. Then it happened.

I hooked something on the third cast. Sometimes when you cast along the carp you end up snagging a carp and this is what I thought I felt. It was little and coming right in to shore without much effort. It didn't fight much at all and came in straight so I then decided it was a small pike.

The fish had not surfaced and came in straight

away. My wife handed me my net and I one-handed the rod with a short amount of line out and put the long handled net in the water. The handle was fully extended and the giant net waited for the fish. My wife had never seen me do this before and she was watching really closely. She was standing to the left of me and peering over the edge of the wall to see what I had hooked. The fish came to the surface with little effort directly alongside my net. My wife shrieked "Oh My God!" when she saw what surfaced. It was that gigantic pike from the season before. All hell broke loose then.

All I can figure is the pike did not realize it was hooked and came to shore because it was hunting for a small carp to eat. When it saw the net it went insane. I was unprepared and not at full strength and caught with my pants down with the rod in one hand and the net in the other.

The biggest pike I had ever seen in my lifetime was on the end of my line with three feet of line out and it was freaking out. It was not tired because of coming in without a battle so it stood up on its tail and made a mighty head shake and threw the lure. I was standing there with my rod in one hand and the net in the other and a stunned look on my face. As we walked back up the bank my wife said something that made me laugh: "Remind me to never wade in the Kickapoo ever again." It brought a smile to my face but I was frowning inside because I was not prepared for the battle. Next year I will be.

USE YOUR HEAD

We met up at 8:30 a.m. He doesn't want me to mention his name because he is a little embarrassed. I will call my friend John. John and I hit the water by 8:45 a.m. The morning was slow but we caught a few trout. John was proud of his new rod and reel. Last year at this time I fished with John and he had a really old rod and matching old reel. I had made fun of it so he went out and got a new one just because I picked on him. He had bought a sturdy rod and reel with the backbone to land some seriously big trout.

John was having some troubles with the new rod. It was like a broom stick, he said. His old rod was fiberglass and very flexible. He was not used to casting this new rod. Many of his casts were in trees and on the bank. John got pretty frustrated by the end of the day and was really reefing on some of his snags to get the lure out. At one time I hid behind John and told him to be careful because his method was poor and dangerous. He was holding onto the line and pulling the snag directly at himself.

As the day progressed and the wind picked up, his casts got even more haphazard and out of control. He was getting more and more frustrated. We started heading back toward John's campground, getting ready to call it quits for the day. There was one hole on the way home right near the road. I told John where to fish one last time. I stayed in the car and watched. John went directly to the hole. On his first cast he snagged his lure. I saw him pulling on his line and the next thing I knew he was kneeling.

I saw him looking around. He was patting the ground looking for something. I assumed his lure had come dislodged and came back at him and fell at his feet. I saw John look around for quite some time. He then grabbed his line and searched for his lure. He followed the line up to his head. The lure had come screaming back at him and gotten stuck in his hat.

He walked back to me at a quick pace. I asked him what was up. He pointed to his cap. I said no big deal unhook it and let's get fishing. John said: "It is not just stuck in the hat."

He got in and looked in the rear view mirror and saw the panther martin hanging from his forehead. A couple meek tugs on the lure failed to dislodge it from his forehead. Then John attempted to cut the treble hook with a big needle nose from my car. This also failed, so off we went to Urgent Care. I asked John if I could take a photo of the injury and he declined. He told me he was quite embarrassed.

We walked into Urgent Care in our waders. John went to the front desk to check in. The receptionist asked him his problem and John pointed at the size 9 panther martin hanging from his forehead. She asked him if he was in pain and he said no. We sat and waited almost a full hour after registering. That was an interesting hour in the waiting room. Every person that came in had to inspect John's shiny panther martin jutting out of his forehead, as if he were the big catch of the day. Somehow people came out of the woodwork to come see the oddity in the waiting room. Reactions were varied. Some smiled and laughed, and others cringed. John was quite embarrassed by the time he finally he got in to see the doctor. Before he went in I asked for a photo again and he declined.

John went in to see the doctor. He once again was the center of attention as news of the unlucky fisherman spread like wildfire throughout the clinic. One by one, all the nurses and medical assistants came to watch the tricky procedure. The doctor tried to cut the treble hook with side cutters with no luck. John even tried with no luck.

Then the doctor got creative. He got out locking

hemostats and secured the treble hook and before John could ask what he was doing the doctor had yanked out the hook. John said it didn't hurt and the doctor put a smiley face band-aid over the small wound and John put back on his cap and recovered his lure. John got a tetanus shot and antibiotics before he left. We went back fishing after our adventure in the clinic. We went to another stream and he was not worse for the injury. We fished the rest of the day and John caught the most browns he had ever caught in a day.

The Bathtub

Many years ago I got permission to fish a local stream at an old farmhouse way back in the boondocks in rural Crawford County. At the time there were an old couple of bachelor brothers that owned the house. They actually lived in another house upstream about 200 yards. This old farmhouse was used by the two as a place to wash up and not dirty up where they lived. You get the gist of what I am saying, right? Their house was a pig pen and not kept up well. I remember getting a glimpse of their downstairs bathroom. There was an old claw-footed bath tub that was filthy. The two gave me permission to fish on their land.

I headed out and I really liked their waterway. It was loaded with eager brook trout.

A couple years went by and one of the brothers had passed so I decided a return trip to the old farmhouse was in order to ask permission again at the beginning of the new trout season. As I drove down the long driveway, I noticed there were significant changes. There was a new name on the mailbox and it looked like the new owners were pig farmers. The stream looked 100 percent different. The pigs had eaten all the vegetation down to nubs and they had free reign to walk in the stream. The place was a mess outside.

I knocked on the door and an older Mennonite woman answered. She gave me permission right away. There was something odd going on in the house. The occupants had moved the claw-footed bathtub to the center of the front room. They had diverted a spring to literally flow in their back door and go into the bathtub then out the front door through PVC piping. It was not my place to ask what they were doing, but it looked odd for a family of six to have a spring diverted through their house.

The next spring I noticed all the PVC pipes in the yard and the bathtub was in an outbuilding. The owner decided to remove his makeshift babbling brook that went directly through his home.

Another year passed and there was another new mailbox on the driveway. It was now white with lady bugs painted on it and a new couple's name was on the box. I had heard a couple from Chicago had moved in and they were private folks. I parked my vehicle way out at the main road and walked down the driveway. I wanted to ask the new owners for permission. Part way down the driveway, I saw a beautiful wooden sign with the couple's names painted on it, and it was adorned with a hand painted woodpecker.

There was music on in the house. It was quite loud so I knew someone was home. I knocked for an extended period of time and no one answered the door. I was about to leave when I heard voices in the back yard. I went to investigate.

I rounded the corner of the back of the house and lo and behold there was that bathtub again. It was sitting in the back of the house with two naked occupants. I looked down at the ground immediately and shielded my eyes. The man was in the back of the tub and his wife was in front of him. As I was shielding my eyes he reached around and covered her best he could with his two hands.

They were both shrieking at me. They wanted to know why I was in their yard. I excused myself and told them I was sorry and all I wanted to do was talk to them about getting permission to trout fish. I told them I would come back another day. The man spoke up and told me I could fish anytime I wanted. I backpedaled around the corner and excused myself again as I did. As I was walking away I heard both of them break in to laughter. The husband yelled from around the house: "No need to be sorry, my wife got a thrill out of it and I am probably going to get lucky because of it!" That didn't set well with the wife and I heard her shout at her husband, "No way is that going to happen!"

I fished for an hour and had good luck. The man came down to introduce himself to me. He had a huge smile on his face the whole time. As I left he said, "YES to your question and smirked and walked away."

The next spring when I came the same owners were there. I couldn't help but notice that there was an addition to their family. The woman was carrying a baby. I talked to both of them for a while and the wife went in the house to feed the child. The man had that same smirk on his face as I left and he told me that his son had been created that day a year ago in the bathtub.

This spring I returned to the home with the bathtub in the yard. The mailbox was different this time. It was weathered and rusted, and only had one name on it. I walked up the driveway and saw the same wooden sign, faded and worn, with the wife's name covered with duct tape. The bathtub was not in the yard anymore. I talked to the male owner and he and I reminisced. It was eighteen years ago that I had caught him and his ex-wife in the bathtub in the yard. Many things had changed since then but he still owned the property. He had moved the bathtub back inside the house. He had hooked it up to regular plumbing and used it as an indoor bathtub. This place had gone through many changes over the years, but the one constant was that old claw-footed bathtub.

Epilogue

I was a little disappointed with my last journey in search of the mythical "Brigadoon Creek." I have a 'three strikes and you're out' superstition. If I fish a stream three times and it fails to produce for me to my expectations, I write it off in my log book as a *"No Return Trip Warranted."*

I had struck out twice in finding the stream of dreams. I thought I should give it one more try. I looked at Google Earth last night until my eyes crossed. I needed one more look to satisfy my curiosity.

I was on the water by 5:20 am. The first hole I came upon looked very fishy. Twenty minutes later and six fish from the hole, I was really fired up. There were two brook trout and four browns standing sentinel at the entrance to "Brigadoon Creek." I can remember thinking to myself: "This is going to be an excellent morning."

The holes were really far apart and any water with twelve inches or more in depth held trout. One hour later and 20 more smallish trout I literally said aloud, *"When is one of these trout going to be photo worthy?"* I have an unwritten rule that a brown trout needs to be fifteen inches to be photo worthy and a brookie needs to be over eleven inches.

I began to question if I had found the magical stream that I heard the old anglers reminiscing about. I rounded a bend in the stream and saw it. The sheer wall the two had described. I was certain I was finally there.

I can remember the two ancient anglers saying, *"There were fish everywhere."* The first cast into this sacred place, the entire hole came to life. There were trout charging at my spinner with blind abandon. They were so eager I did something I had never done with a spinner before. I had two trout on at once. One of the trout got off at hand or I would have taken a photo of the double. I kept track of the fish I landed in that hole. I had twenty four browns to hand and another twenty hits. All trout were less than thirteen inches.

I plodded upstream. I picked up a few more browns. The water got really skinny and then I saw why. There was a huge beaver dam about thirty feet wide and ninety yards long. I was really excited. This large beaver dam was a flop due to lots of weed growth. I caught weeds on every cast. Upstream I went. The stream then forked. I remember the white-haired story tellers saying the left fork went into a totally road free isolated area. It was a no brainer which fork to take. I took the left fork.

The left fork was smaller but it also was six degrees colder. The stream sides were quite jagged and steep. At one place I swear I saw the rock walls of an old structure that might belong in Brigadoon.

The small fork was not as fishy as the main fork. I walked up it quite a ways before I found a pool that could hold trout. The first cast in to the oasis pool I scored a nice brook trout. I picked up a couple more and decided catching any more trout would just be selfish.

It was a long walk back to the car. I had lots of time to think. I replayed what the old gents had said in my mind. "There were trout everywhere" stuck in my head. They said trout everywhere NOT big trout everywhere. This stream was their stream of dreams.

I caught my first trout at a young age. My father had set it up for me and it was caught on my first cast as a five-year-old first time trout angler. This trout was huge. It measured 23 and 3/4 inches. My whole way of thinking about trout fishing was formed that first day. I look at trout fishing differently than most.

One angler's Brigadoon Creek can be another angler's Average Creek. I have always said, "I would trade twenty small trout for one big trout." I am still in search of my *Brigadoon Creek.* The creek of my dreams is still out there. I will never give up looking for it. And I did not dismiss this creek completely. An early season trip to that long beaver dam may be a hidden gem. In early season the weeds have not grown up and this may change things for the better. There could be size and numbers. This would make it everyone's *Brigadoon Creek.* I still have hope that I will find my stream of dreams before it disappears into the mist forever.

We trout anglers are dreamers.

About the Author

Len Harris is a dreamer.

"About three months ago I made a comment to an acquaintance about trout fishing being so important to me, and he dismissed it. He said trout fishing was the least important thing he does in life and I shouldn't make it so important. I wholeheartedly disagree with him. Many people go to church to feel spiritual and be in touch with the universe. I go into the outdoors to cleanse my soul. All the things in life that bother me are melted away about a hundred yards from the truck. The fish are only a bonus in the whole scheme of things."

Made in the USA
San Bernardino, CA
31 July 2014